T0025821

LEVEL
1
YOU READ · I READ

Cats

Joan Marie Galat

NATIONAL
GEOGRAPHIC

Washington, D.C.

How to Use This Book

Reading together is fun! When older and younger readers share the experience, it opens the door to new learning. As you read together, talk about what you learn.

This side is for a parent, older sibling, or older friend. Before reading each page, take a look at the words and pictures. Talk about what you see. Point out words that might be hard for the younger reader.

This side is for the younger reader.

As you read, look for the bolded words. Talk about them before you read. In each chapter, the bolded words are:
Chapter 1: descriptive words • Chapter 2: body parts
Chapter 3: action words • Chapter 4: action words

At the end of each chapter, do the activity together.

YOUR TURN!

Look at each part of the cat's body and match it with the correct word.

teeth

whiskers

claws

tail

Table of Contents

Big Cats and Little Cats

Cats hide and sneak, then leap and pounce. All cats are meat-eaters with sharp teeth and claws. But cats can also be very different. Some are **tame** and others are wild.

 House cats are called **tame** because they are gentle and not afraid of people.

YOU READ

Other cats are **wild.** There are 36 types of wild cats. They live around the world, except for in Australia, Antarctica, and on some islands. Wild cats eat, sleep, and raise their young in an area called a home range.

Wild cats guard the area where they live. They often live far from people.

Wild cats can be very big or very **small.** The rusty-spotted cat can weigh as little as a pineapple—about two pounds. It often climbs to the top of a rock or tree and then listens for prey below. It hunts birds, small mammals, frogs, lizards, and insects.

 This **small** cat is
a fast climber.
It can run up a
tree to stay safe.

YOU
READ
Some large cats belong to a group called the big cats. Leopards, jaguars, and lions are big cats, but tigers are the largest. A tiger can weigh up to 700 pounds—almost as **heavy** as four men.

 A leopard isn't the biggest cat, but it's strong. It can carry **heavy** prey up a tree.

Wild cats need a habitat with a water source and enough food to hunt. They live in both hot and cold places, including deserts, jungles, grasslands, forests, and mountains. Both big and small wild cats are **skilled** at taking care of themselves. They find what they need to survive.

Tame cats are **skilled** at finding what they need, too. They live with people but still know how to hunt for food.

YOUR TURN!

Cats can be tame or wild. How can you tell which cats live with people and which cats are wild?

CHAPTER 2

A Cat's Body

Whether they are big or small, wild or tame, all cats are skilled hunters. Sharp **teeth** and claws help them capture prey. A mammal, bird, or fish will make a tasty meal.

Some cats hunt big animals. Four big front **teeth** help them catch their prey.

Most cats can push out their **claws** to hunt. They use their curved claws to capture and hold prey. They also use their claws to dig into the ground. That helps them run faster.

I READ A cat's sharp **claws** grab on to a tree trunk. This helps the cat climb up and up.

19

Cats use their **tail** to balance. Turning their tail different ways can help cats climb, leap, or walk across a tree branch or fence. If they fall, cats almost always land on their feet.

Cheetahs turn their **tail** when they run. This helps them change direction quickly.

YOU READ Cats get a lot of information from their **whiskers.** The long hairs can feel nearby objects. Whiskers can tell a cat the size of a mouse's hole. They help cats find their way in the dark, too.

Whiskers can feel tiny changes in the air. This tells a cat when prey is on the move!

YOUR TURN!

Look at each part of the cat's body and match it with the correct word.

teeth

whiskers

claws

tail

A

B

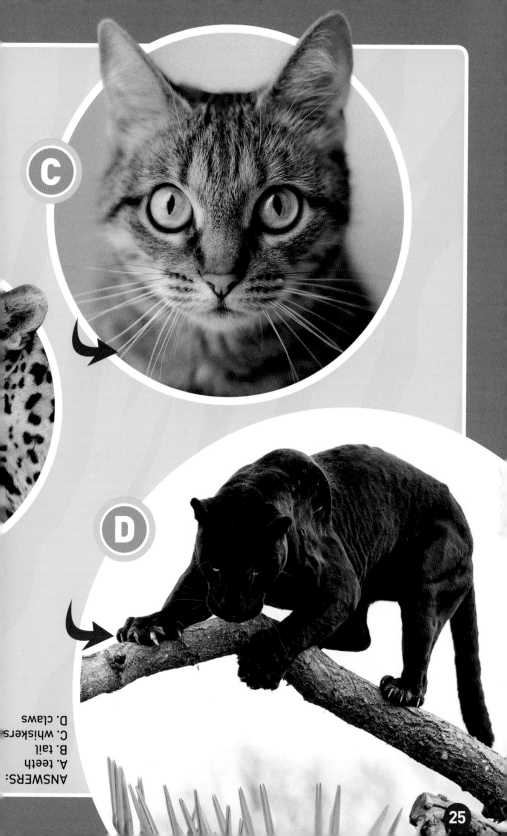

C

D

CHAPTER 3

Survival

YOU
READ

Wild cats can survive in different parts of the world. Canada lynx live in northern forests. Large paws help them walk over deep snow to **look** for prey. The paws act like snowshoes so they don't sink into the snow.

 Lynx travel many miles every day to **look** for food. Their thick winter coats keep them warm.

 The fishing cat lives near swamps, streams, and rivers. It searches for its food in water. Webs on the cat's front feet help it **swim** after prey. Large claws help it hold slippery fish.

I READ Fishing cats can **swim** underwater. Their thick fur keeps them dry.

YOU READ

Sand cats live in the desert. The sand is hot to step on, but sand cats have long, thick hairs on the bottom of their paws. The hairs **protect** their paws from heat as the cats travel across the sand.

Sand cats have soft, thick fur. Their coat **protects** them from hot days and cold nights.

Cheetahs can be found in open areas and grasslands. The fastest animals on land, cheetahs have bodies that are built to run. They have long legs and light bones that help them **sprint** toward their prey.

Cheetahs slowly sneak up close to their prey. Then they **sprint** at top speed!

33

Whether they are big or small, most cats prefer to live and **hunt** alone. The African lion is different. Between 3 and 40 lions may live together in a pride.

 The lions **hunt** together. Teamwork helps them survive.

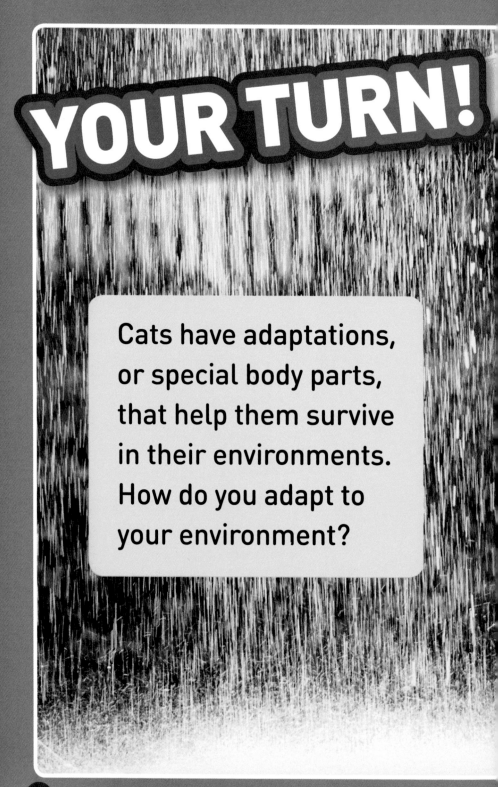

YOUR TURN!

Cats have adaptations, or special body parts, that help them survive in their environments. How do you adapt to your environment?

CHAPTER 4

Cat Talk

Cats communicate to let other cats know when they should stay away and when it is OK to come close. They use sounds, movements, and smells to send messages. Cats may growl or bare their teeth. Some cats send a signal when they **scratch** tree trunks.

Some cats leave a smell when they **scratch.**
The smell means the cat lives here.

Some wild cats make loud sounds to send messages to other animals. Lions **roar** to communicate with other cats and to warn them, "Stay away. This is my space."

Lions **roar** when they have food to protect. Some other animals may try to grab a bite.

Cats use body movements to send messages without making a sound. The end of a leopard's tail twitches when it spots prey or feels excited. A leopard will **raise** its tail to lead cubs through tall grass. The white tip on the leopard's tail makes it easy to see.

Some wild cats **raise** their tail when they greet each other. Others rub cheeks to say hello.

House cats share messages, too. They hold their body a certain way or make a face that shows if they are happy or relaxed. Adult cats **meow** to share messages with people. A meow may mean "Hello" or "Look at the mouse I caught."

 A **meow** can also mean "Feed me!" Wild cats and tame cats both make sounds to get what they need. They are alike in many ways!

YOUR TURN!

Look at each cat's actions. What do you think the cat is saying?

For Justine, with love. —J. M. G.

Published by National Geographic Partners, LLC, Washington, DC 20036.

Designed by YAY! Design

The author and publisher gratefully acknowledge the expert content review of this book by Linda Sweanor, wild cat biologist and past president of Wild Felid Research and Management Association, and the literacy review of this book by Kimberly Gillow, Principal, Milan Area Schools, Michigan.

Library of Congress Cataloging-in-Publication Data

Names: Galat, Joan Marie, 1963- author. | National Geographic Society (U.S.)
Title: Cats / Joan Marie Galat.
Description: Washington, DC : National Geographic, [2017] | Series: National geographic reader | Audience: Ages 2-5. | Audience: Preschool, excluding K.
Identifiers: LCCN 2016051366 (print) | LCCN 2017020788 (ebook) | ISBN 9781426328855 (e-book) | ISBN 9781426328831 (pbk. : alk. paper) | ISBN 9781426328848 (hardcover : alk.paper)
Subjects: LCSH: Felidae--Juvenile literature. | Cats--Juvenile literature.
Classification: LCC QL737.C23 (ebook) | LCC QL737.C23 G3544 2017 (print) | DDC 599.75--dc23
LC available at https://lccn.loc.gov/2016051366

Cats in the book
Cover: house cats; 1: ocelot; 3: house cat; 4: leopard; 5: house cat; 6: (UP LE) Canada lynx, (UP RT) lion, (LO) serval; 7: tiger; 8–9: rusty-spotted cats; 10: Bengal tiger; 11: African leopard; 12: cheetahs; 13: house cats; 14: (LE) ocelot, (RT) house cat; 15: (UP LE) house cat, (UP RT) Bengal tiger, (CTR) lion, (LO) house cat; 16: house cat; 17: lion; 18: clouded leopard; 19: caracal; 20: house cat; 21: cheetah; 22: house cat; 23: Scottish wildcat; 24: (UP) jaguar, (LO) leopard; 25: (UP) house cat, (LO) jaguar; 26–27: lynx; 28–29: fishing cats; 30–31: sand cats; 32–33: cheetahs; 34–35: lions; 38: (LE) puma, (RT) house cat; 39: tiger; 40–41: lions; 42: leopard; 43: tigers; 44–45: house cats; 46: leopard; 47: (UP) house cat, (CTR) house cat, (LO) lion

Illustration Credits
Cover, Klein-Hubert/Kimball Stock; 1, Pete Oxford/Minden Pictures; 3, kot2626/Getty Images; 4, Aditya Singh/Getty Images; 5, Glow Images, Inc/Getty Images; 6 (UP LE), Michael Quinton/Minden Pictures; 6 (UP RT), ajlber/Getty Images; 6 (LO), FionaAyerst/Getty Images; 7, Steve Winter/National Geographic Image Collection; 8, Edwin Giesbers/Nature Picture Library; 9, Arco Images GmbH/Alamy Stock Photo; 10 (UP), Anan Kaewkhammul/Shutterstock; 10 (LO), aldomurillo/Getty Images; 11, Jeff Mauritzen; 12, Jami Tarris/Getty Images; 13, Benjamin Torode/Getty Images; 14 (LE), Pete Oxford/Minden Pictures; 14 (RT), KidStock/Getty Images; 14-15 (background), Dzmitry Kim/Shutterstock; 15 (UP LE), SaNa/Shutterstock; 15 (UP RT), Steve Winter/National Geographic Image Collection; 15 (CTR), Maultby2005/Getty Images; 15 (LO), John Daniels/ARDEA; 16, CameronGallant/Getty Images; 17, Tier Und Naturfotografie J und C Sohns/Getty Images; 18, Mark Newman/Getty Images; 18 (inset), Picture by Tambako the Jaguar/Getty Images; 19, BirdImages/Getty Images; 20, tomch/Getty Images; 21, Gallo Images - Martin Harvey/Getty Images; 22, Seregraff/Getty Images; 23, DavidCallan/Getty Images; 24 (UP), Bruno Pambour/Biosphoto; 24 (LO), Andy Rouse/NPL/Minden Pictures; 24-25 (background), Dzmitry Kim/Shutterstock; 25 (UP), kapulya/Getty Images; 25 (LO), Picture by Tambako the Jaguar/Getty Images; 26-27, Paul Sawer/Minden Pictures; 26 (inset), Frank Pali/Getty Images; 28 (inset), Arco Images GmbH/Alamy Stock Photo; 28-29, wrangel/Getty Images; 30, Picture by Tambako the Jaguar/Getty Images; 31 (LE), Photononstop/Alamy Stock Photo; 31 (RT), Thomas Rabeil/Minden Pictures; 32, NHPA/Superstock; 33, Alex Hibbert/Getty Images; 34-35, Nigel Pavitt/John Warburton-Lee Photography Ltd/Getty Images; 35 (inset), Per-Gunnar Ostby/Getty Images; 36-37, Jim Cummins/Getty Images; 38 (LE), Frank Lukasseck/Getty Images; 38 (RT), Jana Horova/Shutterstock; 39, imageBROKER/Alamy Stock Photo; 40, Delta Images/Getty Images; 41, Keren Su/Getty Images; 42, Jami Tarris/Getty Images; 43, Marion Vollborn/Minden Pictures; 44, Laurie Rubin/Getty Images; 45, Jean-Philippe Tournut/Getty Images; 46, Richard Wear/Getty Images; 46-47 (background), Dzmitry Kim/Shutterstock; 47 (UP LE), liveostockimages/Getty Images; 47 (UP RT), Image by Chris Winsor/Getty Images; 47 (LO), Dominique Delfino/Getty Images; (header throughout), Pavel Hlystov/Shutterstock

Printed in the United States of America
22/WOR/5 (PB)
22/WOR/4 (RLB)